Wild, Wild 1950s Cookies

First Edition
03 02 01 00 99   5 4 3 2 1

Published by
Gibbs Smith, Publisher
P.O. Box 667
Layton, Utah 84041
E-mail: info@gibbs-smith.com
Website: www.gibbs-smith.com

Design by J. Scott Knudsen, Park City, Utah
Photography by Jan Shou,
    Borge B. Anderson & Associates, Inc.,
    Salt Lake City

Printed and bound in Hong Kong

**Library of Congress
    Cataloging-in-Publication Data**
Crews, Tuda Libby, 1943–
Wild, wild 1950s cookies / Tuda Libby
    Crews.
p. cm.
ISBN 0-87905-893-5
1. Cookies. I. Title.
TX772.C685   1999
641.8'654—DC21   98-45263
                        CIP

WILD, WILD 1950s Cookies

Tada Libby Crews

AUTHOR OF
Wild, Wild West Cowboy Cookies

GIBBS·SMITH
P
PUBLISHER

SALT LAKE CITY

Acknowledgments

Several years ago when publisher Gibbs Smith became interested in my Wild, Wild Cookie cookbook series, a variety of ideas for themes had occurred to me. I mentioned some of them to my daughter, Libby, and she interrupted with, "Mother, you need to do the *Wild, Wild 1950s Cookies,* and you should include those wonderful black-and-white photos of your 4-H baking demonstration!" So here is your favorite Wild, Wild Cookie cookbook idea, Libby, and I thank you and love you dearly. As you were growing up, I cherish the many polkas we danced as I made my way toward the kitchen. I look forward to decorating pink poodles and saddle shoes and jukeboxes with Bella. When I have blue hair and walk with a cane, I'll drive her to country dances.

Thank you, Ted, for giving me such motherly joy and pride in your many accomplishments. Thanks, too, for sharing your creative marketing ability and for your patience with my ever-lagging computer skills. You're the *best* counsel I have, and I love you, son.

I appreciate my family, champions of this new cookie career that often draws each of them, even my friend Peter Wood, into my swirling vortex of baking and decorating cookies for weddings, parties, fund-raisers, or book signings. I especially thank my husband, Jack, who waits for me to return to our little ranch house from various book-promotion efforts, and often keeps dinner warm on the stove. You're "a good man" and I love you for it.

And to my extraordinary and patient mother, Esther Libby, thank you for giving "us Girls" the joy of two-stepping and jitterbugging through the 1950s. It was the *grooviest* time of my life!

Warm thanks to my editor, Madge Baird, for her appreciation and support of this project, and to Linda Nimori for technical editing. Our creative team includes clever food stylist Caroll Shreeve, who designed the layouts of fancy-dancy '50s icons and shimmering sugar-coated cookies. And Jan Shou's extraordinary photography makes every Wild, Wild 1950s cookie fairly jitterbug to life with vibrant color for book designer J. Scott Knudsen to wrap his creative arms around. Scott's imagination and genius have put the fun into this book that, for me, brings back an era worth celebrating at any age. Thanks, too, for the love and support from all my dear friends and advisors along the way, including Owaissa Crites Heimann and Foster Zimmerman—top-notch extension agents—and close friend Shorty Jenkins, who positively influenced my personal growth in the 1950s.

Contents

Introduction 7

PART ONE: RECIPES 16
Doughs 18
    Jukebox Gingies 18
    Bobby Socks Scotchies 19
    Cherry Chocolate Cokies 20
Frostings 21
    Cherry Chocolate Frosting 21
    Boogie-Woogie Butterscotch Frosting 22
    Royal Icing 22

PART TWO: TIPS & TECHNIQUES 23
Doughs—Handling & Baking 24
    Chilling Tips 24
    Rolling-out Tips 25
    Cutting-out Tips 26
    Baking Tips 27
    Bebop-a-loo-a Tips 27
Frostings—Preparing & Applying 28
    Fun Ideas 28
        Fabulous '50s Food 28
        Groovy Cookie Clothes 30
        Marvelously Misty Memories 32
    Supplies 34
    Coloring Tips 35
    Background Techniques 36
    Piped-on Details 38
Cookies—Storing & Shipping 41

PART THREE: TOOLS, TRANSFERS & SOURCES 42
Using Transfers 44
Finding Sources 45
    Products 45
    Concerts 45
    Recordings 45
Arranging Demonstrations & Workshops 46
Ordering Wild 1950s Cookie Cutters 47

To "the Girls." This book is dedicated
to my sisters, Tacey Libby Levis and
Mary Libby Campbell, and my first
cousin, Sydney Lou Farlow Day, who
grew up with us in the 1950s back at
the ranch. May we always be
remembered as "the Girls."

To all you lovers of the wild and wonderful 1950s, I hope this second in my series of cookie books inspires you to come with me via sugar, butter, flour, and vanilla to re-create the era. From the remote vantage point of northeastern New Mexico, not far from Route 66, come these charming, toothsome 1950s confections. I hope you'll gather up some Elvis Presley, Buddy Holly and the Crickets, Bill Haley and the Comets, and Fats Domino tunes and some kids to accompany your cookie making. And don't be afraid to teach the kids how to dance—really dance! Gather in the kitchen to bake and decorate pink poodles and blue suede shoes and jukeboxes. Tell your '50s stories. I love telling mine.

This book is in memory of a jitterbugging, two-stepping, smooching, skin-tight-jeans-and-bobby-sock-wearing era.

Growing up on a ranch in New Mexico during the '50s, I liked my position as the middle child of five siblings. Someone told me that being the middle child was akin to the filling in a sandwich—the best part—and I agree. We kids were raised to work hard, love one another, and feed our neighbors in the spirit of kindness. Out of that spirit was born my dedication to preparing and serving good food. Mother always said, "Food is love made visible."

Our 1950s lifestyle on our isolated ranch was different from that of urban teenagers; we had no television, telephone, or music lessons. (Nobody had even thought of computers or video games back then.) In high school, our winter days were filled with forty-mile drives—each way—to attend school in Amistad. We returned home to the ranch after school at 5:00 P.M., nearly dusk.

Mother or Grandma Baca *always* had delicious homemade food waiting for us. The warm ovens and fragrant baking aromas drew us to the kitchen for snacks, and their listening ears kept us there chatting about the day's activities. There were apple dumplings served with thick fresh cream, warm banana bread spread with a half-inch layer of chocolate frosting sprinkled with chopped walnuts, or applesauce spice cookies studded with pecans. I especially recall times we could sample Grandma Baca's fresh raised doughnuts that were coated with a fragile sugar glaze and covered every countertop in the kitchen. Refueled, we changed clothes, then went outside for chores.

We fed, cleaned stalls, brushed our calves, and filled the water tanks. In winter, it was always dark by the time we finished our work. We were starving by then and ready for our family supper, after which we did the dishes together.

7

Following homework, we went to bed, then got up at 5:30 the next morning to go through the same routine again. We never questioned what we were doing, we just did what needed to be done.

We were all involved in 4-H, an agriculture enrichment program designed for rural families. We were influenced by outstanding extension agents Owaissa Crites and Foster Zimmerman. Our mother served as a 4-H Leader and was instrumental in teaching us sewing, cooking, public speaking, and presenting 4-H demonstrations. Daddy paid all the bills. We ran high-quality Hereford cows on our ranch

and had the opportunity to select from the top calves in the herd for our 4-H projects. Our big brother, Chappy, was very supportive in overseeing our calf projects. To give our 4-H calves a mile of exercise a day, we rigged up a long pipe attached behind the tractor and welded hooks on it. We tied the calves to the hooks and walked eight head of fat steers at one time. Regardless of the weather, our little brother, Junior, was the stalwart driver. Our steers usually placed high at the

county fair and then competed at the state fair in Albuquerque. I remember once at the state fair, I went into the 4-H Youth Hall to have breakfast and happened to sit across the table from my lifelong cowboy idol, Roy Rogers. It was one of the biggest thrills of my life!

In 1958 my Slice and Serve Cookies won the 4-H Cooking Demonstration contest at State 4-H Camp, which was held on the campus at New Mexico State University. My mother and dad would get a charge to know that my 4-H experience set the stage for a veritable cookie career! At State Camp we dressed in poodle skirts and bobby socks. Between breaks, we country kids hotfooted it over to a college-student hangout called the Canteen, fed quarters into the jukebox, and danced the jitterbug to "Wake Up, Little Susie," or two-stepped to "City Lights." If someone asked us to dance, we danced. We *never* said "no, thank you," even if we'd never seen the person before. Often we danced with each other just for the pure joy of dancing! Our adorable baby sister, Mary, could dance as soon as she learned to walk. Also, if there were cute boys around, we sometimes used her as a messenger to invite them over to meet us. Sometimes we used her as bait just to draw attention to us Girls. Little Mary became very proficient at flirting and coyly directing the guys our way.

Our cousin, Sydney Lou, who was like a sister to us, and Tacey and I spent a lot of time together. In those days we gave each other home perms, debating on which brand yielded the softest curl—Toni or Richard Hudnut. We carefully applied Helena Rubenstein makeup and plucked our eyebrows thin. We wore fabulous clip-on earrings so large they covered our ears. Clothes were important to us Girls. For casual occasions we wore Ship 'n' Shore blouses with round Peter Pan collars, cuffed our Levi's, and wore bobby socks and saddle shoes. Our mother bought us beautiful, expensive clothes from family friend Jess Zurick, who owned the Frock Shoppe in Tucumcari near Route 66.

We Girls were young when we learned to sew. I started sewing at age ten and was soon turning out gathered skirts and pedal pushers. By fourteen, I was skilled enough to sew fully lined, tailored wool, Chanel-style suits with straight skirts. Mother fed our creative spirits and bought not yards but *miles* of wonderful fabrics, laces, and trim. We soon outgrew Mother's little black portable Singer, so Daddy bought us Girls a new Necchi Elna automatic sewing machine. Tacey was a fabulous designer and seamstress, and she created adorable original outfits for our

baby sister, Mary. At age five, Mary wore a huge turquoise-and-silver concha belt with snug-fitting western bell-bottom trousers. Tacey made us dozens of rickrack-trimmed broomstick skirts, embellished men's shirts with lavish laces, and created stunning original fashions for us Girls to wear.

The annual 4-H Dress Review gave us all a chance to boast our sewing skills as we modeled our sophisticated outfits accessorized with kid gloves and handsome leather handbags. Our shoes were stiletto-spiked heels, and we wore pillbox hats with little dotted veils. We were properly underpinned in Playtex girdles held in place by seamed stockings attached to dangling garters. Our bosoms were high and pointing in our Warner three-way cotton bras, under-wired for donning halter tops or strapless formals.

We often dressed alike. My favorite trio tops were Christian Dior knockoffs in bold black-and-white-striped cotton with bateau necklines and dropped sleeves. We wore the pullovers, tapered to fit snug around our hips, on the outside of our skin-tight Levi's. The plastered fit of our jeans was achieved by wearing brand new Levi's in a tub filled with very hot water and lying there for thirty minutes. We got out of the tub dripping wet and wore the Levi's until they were completely air-dried. Mr. Strauss would have had heart failure if he could have seen our lower extremities colored navy blue from the dyes he used in those days. Sometimes our Levi's fit so tight we had to lie on the bed and use a pair of pliers and a coat hanger to button up our pants.

Easily entertained on trips to town, we loved to drag Main at any hour of the day, and we'd wave at the cute boys who worked at gas stations up and down the street. I believe our dad's greatest fear was that we would marry a gas-pump jockey. The cute guys that pumped gas on the Route 66 strip in Tucumcari, seventy-five miles from the ranch, called us "The Fabulous Libby Sisters"—and that really turned our heads.

When it came to Elvis, though, we were plumb giddy. Sydney Lou was born on Elvis's birthday—the lucky hound dog! I remember we wore Levi's and our matching black-and-white-striped tops to the Luna Theater in Clayton to watch our heart-throb star in *Jailhouse Rock.* Every time Elvis sang and wriggled his hips on the screen, we wept and screamed; our

hearts just pounded right out of our little bodies from 1:30 in the afternoon until 10:30 that night. (Mr. Murphy didn't empty the theater after each showing, so we certainly got our 25 cents worth of entertainment.) To this day, my heart goes pitty-pat when I hear Elvis's music.

We loved ice-cream sodas and banana splits and usually stopped for treats before heading home. In those days drugstores had counters with tall stools and marble-trimmed mirrors over the stainless-steel ice-cream freezers. Teens earned extra money as soda jerks, dishing up delectable treats such as butterscotch sundaes and chocolate sodas. Kids went to the drugstore to talk, flirt, and make weekend plans. The hamburger drive-ins had portable juke-boxes that pulled forward to rest along-side the car window. One of our favorite songs was Marty Robbins's "A White Sport

Coat and a Pink Carnation." Friendly carhops in short skirts made time to chat as they placed our orders on the attached window tray. We ate divine greasy hamburgers and french fries with lots of ketchup, all served in red plastic woven baskets. We drank cherry sodas in frosty cold glasses.

When our ranch house was remodeled, Daddy bought us Girls a modern blond-oak RCA Victrola three-speed record player. It played stacks of 78s and 33s all day long. During the summer, each morning we selected long-playing albums, from Chet Atkins, Johnny Ray, and Teresa Brewer to the rousing sounds of the "Beer Barrel Polka," and we rocked! We often captured our chuckling mother emerging from the ranch office and danced a fast polka with her across the living-room floor—one two three, hop! one two three, hop!—and steered her into the kitchen where she would breathlessly set about mixing twenty pounds of flour into ranch rolls or put beans on to cook.

I loved branding, the most important event of each summer. Long days working in the hot sun began with a 4:00 A.M. breakfast of bacon, eggs, and biscuits. By 5:00, the cowboys rode out to gather the bawling cows and calves from the pastures and herd them into corrals. The Circle Bar brand was centered on the calf's right rib to identify it as part of our herd.

We often fed more than forty people at mealtime. Noon meal preparations began early in the morning; then the food was loaded into the red-and-white Jeep and driven out to the branding corral before noon. One day we'd be at Flo Camp, another day at the Wire Corrals. To me, every day was a feast. The menu always included succulent roast beef, pinto beans and red chili, good potatoes, salads, hot rolls and Mother's delicious desserts, such as peach cobbler or chocolate cake. On the last day, we'd finish up branding at our home place, and it was a real social event with lots of laughter and stories. In the afternoon, the womenfolk brought over extra desserts, with at least one made from a recipe calling for exotic combinations of Jell-O and canned fruit. Sometimes we'd even churn homemade ice cream to go with Mother's chocolate cake.

Fairs, rodeos, and country dances provided other summer fun. Mother drove us everywhere because she loved for us to have a good time. Often the distance was greater than a hundred miles one way. In my adult years, I've marveled at my mother's patience. Sometimes she sat inside and watched us dance, passing the time visiting with friends. Often she curled up and napped in the car, and we would wake her when the dance was over and it was time to leave. I can still hear the powerful motor of our two-toned white and pea-green chrome-trimmed 1956 Buick roaring down the highway as we headed back to the ranch. I recall a Saturday night when she drove us back from a dance in Boice City, Oklahoma —we didn't get home until about 7:30 in the morning. We Girls were concerned that Daddy might be a tad upset. The minute we got home we three jumped under the covers with our clothes on and pretended to be asleep. Mother cleverly managed to let him think she had been home for quite a while. A few minutes later, Daddy opened the door to our room and said in a low voice, "They must have rolled up the sidewalks last night." I love that saying; in my memory I envision tight

FIREBALLS, a registered trademark

rolls of gray concrete happily standing at the corners of every block on either side of Main Street, like little soldiers in a salute to the early pink of a quiet Sunday dawn.

At Rigoni's in Roy, a small town about forty miles from the ranch, we danced in a big hall on a slick hardwood floor to a band called the Fireballs. We adored the guys and traveled great distances to jitterbug to their music. One time after a dance, Mother let the Fireballs drive us home. I don't remember what kind of car it was, but I do remember it was very crowded with all the band instruments and us Girls packed inside. When we got to the house in the wee hours of the morning, Mother served fried chicken and scrambled eggs. We had hot biscuits with cream gravy and some of her famous German chocolate cake for dessert. After breakfast, we went into the big living room, cranked up the Victrola, and danced until Daddy appeared in his Bermuda-length summer pj's (we were mortified!) and bellered at those boys to go home.

One time we talked Mother into driving us to Clovis, about ninety miles from the ranch, and she waited for us

the entire evening at the bus depot. We had been invited to watch the Fireballs record a new song at the Norman Petty Studio. I remember that, after the session and a tour of the Studio, the Fireballs took us to ride go-carts, which I had never heard of. Now the Fireballs have reunited and play gigs all over the U.S. for audiences who remember all the words to those hit songs and who rock along to the rhythm of "Torquay" and "Bulldog." And George Tomsco, my longtime Fireballs friend, inspired the idea for a "Sugar Shack" cookie.

Forty years after tight jeans and twisting in a ranch-house living room till dawn, we again danced to the Fireballs' music at the seventy-fifth anniversary of Harding County, New Mexico. In the summer of 1997, Tacey, Sydney Lou, Mary, and I gussied up and drove to the small town of Roy in Tacey's brand-new red sports car for a big celebration at the Community Center. (Mary, now a wife and mother, is the fulcrum of our sister relationship. Petite and vivacious as ever, she's still a fabulous dancer; however, she barely tolerates us calling her "little Mary," even though it still seems natural to Sydney Lou, Tacey, and me.) We arrived at the dance earlier than our husbands, and when they came in, they asked, "Where are the Girls?" We were up on the stage getting reacquainted with the Fireballs! We danced every dance. If our men tired out on us, we jitterbugged and waltzed with each other, just as we had danced together in the 1950s. At 2:00 A.M., we cooked a delicious bacon-and-egg breakfast back at the ranch. As we watched the sunrise, we sat around the table talking and giggling about how some things never change.

The 1950s era remains a bright spot. It was a productive time for our country; I remember that cattle prices came up and Daddy was grateful. The *Saturday Evening Post* and *Life* magazine brought photojournalism into our home, keeping us abreast of world news. President Dwight D. Eisenhower was our respected leader, but we stocked a bomb shelter area in our basement just in case. The NASA space program was dreaming of going to the moon . . . I wondered if they'd ever make it. Home television was introduced, but it was Fibber McGee & Molly and the Lone Ranger & Tonto who provided evening family entertainment around the radio. We didn't hear or use four-letter words. Air travel was limited; I was seventeen before I flew in a plane. Almost everyone smoked cigarettes, but grass was mowed and pot meant something you cooked in and Coke was only a cold drink. Movie stars were a big part of our lives; Eddie Fisher & Debbie Reynolds, Tony Curtis & Janet Leigh symbolized model American couples. Marlon Brando and James Dean were rebels, and Marilyn Monroe was the temptress of the times. I loved Doris Day, Clark Gable, and Jimmy Stewart. John Wayne was everyone's hero, most especially my mother's. We Girls played Old Maid and

checkers and did the hoola-hoop and danced by the hours. The music—oh, how it lifted your feet to the rhythm of the beat and made you wanna dance! Like my daughter, Libby, I still nurture a deep infatuation with the fifties era. I've saved everything, from my handmade cowboy boots to strapless formals, and most especially, *the memories.*

Now, we Girls are border-line senior citizens, a segment of the baby-boomer era we used to read about. We have adult children and grandchildren. We still have fun together. We dust off some of those old 78 and 45 records and boogie to the toe-tapping rhythm of Buddy Holly's "Peggy Sue" and Little Richard's "Ready, Teddy" . . . and you can, too! I recently took care of our six-month-old granddaughter, Isabelle Skye Wood, whom we call Bella. Even though she was too young to decorate cookies, I cranked up the volume really loud to Elvis Presley's CD and Bella squealed with delight as I held her and danced in the kitchen to "All Shook Up." Remember, it is very, very important to pass down to the children your favorite family recipes and your best-loved family traditions.

ookie baker "alert" for all of you precious angels . . .

The world needs more cookie bakers. Cookie bakers give away their time and talent in a true labor of love by mixing, baking, and decorating beautiful cookies. Cookie bakers are angels who bring folks together to establish family traditions and create lasting memories in the minds of children and close friends; they touch hearts with delight when cookies are shared. And because they are so very special, cookie bakers deserve good equipment. To make cookie baking an easier and more joyful experience, invest in a heavy-duty Kitchen Aid mixer. Good baking pans prevent cookies from scorching or burning, so buy at least four heavy-gauge aluminum pans that measure 12 x 17 inches. I prefer the pans that have edges about 1 inch high. These multipurpose pans bake perfect cookies and also work for baking sheet cakes, jelly rolls, and large batches of brownies. Lining the cookie sheets with parchment paper makes the cleanup a breeze. Buy at least four extra-large metal wire racks for cooling cookies, and invest in a marble rolling pin. The marble remains cool and helps keep chilled dough from softening. There, cookie bakers, I've given you permission to treat yourselves, and you deserve it.

Plan ahead before you make cookies. Read the recipe in advance to make sure you have all ingredients on hand. Use pure vanilla extract and fresh ingredients in your cookies. Do not overmix the dough at any stage in the process. Measure ingredients accurately; if you alter a recipe, expect an altered finished product. Because all bakers measure a little differently, experience is the best teacher in learning the *feel* of good cookie dough. Use the *touch test*. If your finished dough doesn't stick together in the mixing bowl, knead in a few teaspoons of warm water to make it more pliable. If the dough sticks to your fingers when you touch it, add flour (¼ cup at a time) until it passes the "touch test."

Note: *Touch test—if your fingers can press the dough, leave an indentation, and come away clean, the*

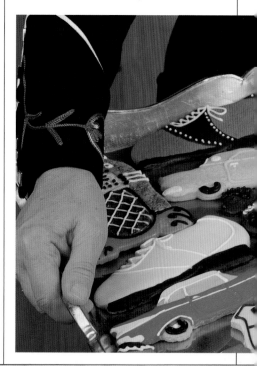

16

dough is ready for chilling.

All three cookie-dough recipes make large batches and require using a heavy-duty mixer or food processor. The recipes are easily cut in half for a small electric mixer or for mixing by hand. It is less work when you mix, cut out, and bake the cookies in advance of decorating them. Undecorated cookies freeze well.

Note: *For the tastiest flavorings, purchase LorAnn Oils from the Finding Sources list on page 45.*

Pay special attention to Part II: Tips & Techniques on pages 23–41. For example, rolling out the dough between layers of wide plastic wrap is different from the traditional method of handling dough. To achieve professional-looking cookies, master this technique.

Note: *All three cookie dough recipes may be stored frozen for up* to six weeks. *Carefully stack plastic-wrapped rolled-out sheets of dough and place in large freezer bags. After freezing, allow dough to thaw overnight in the refrigerator before rolling out.*

For best results in achieving the perfect cookie from this point on, follow instructions on pages 23–27, Part II (Doughs—Handling & Baking).

When you are ready to decorate the cookies, mix and color the frosting a day in advance. On the day you decorate, invite children and friends to join in. Planning makes cookie decorating fun for everyone, including you. Keep cookies on hand at all times; undecorated, they freeze very well in an airtight container.

Note: *Before coloring frosting or decorating cookies, read pages 28–39, Part II (Frostings—Preparing & Applying).*

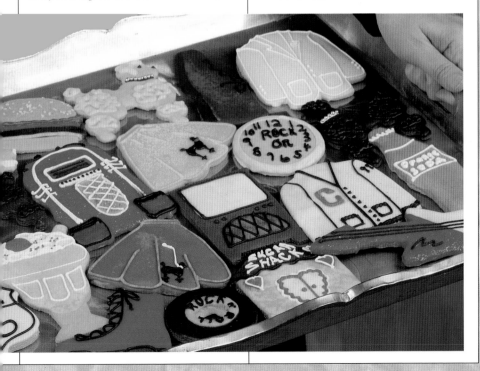

Jukebox Gingies

Put quarters in the jukebox and boogie to the beat of your favorite '50s tunes while making these moist and delicious ginger-flavored cookies that store beautifully.

7¾ cups all-purpose flour
2 teaspoons baking soda
½ teaspoon salt
2½ teaspoons ground ginger
4 teaspoons ground cinnamon
1 teaspoon allspice
1 teaspoon ground cardamom
1 teaspoon freshly grated nutmeg
¾ cup salted butter, room temperature
1 cup butter-flavored vegetable shortening
2 teaspoons pure vanilla extract
1½ cups unsulfured molasses
2 large eggs
2 cups dark-brown sugar, packed

Measure and sift the flour into a large mixing bowl. Measure soda, salt, ginger, cinnamon, allspice, cardamom, and nutmeg, and add to the flour. Using a wire whisk, thoroughly mix the dry ingredients and set aside.

Cream together the butter and shortening until well mixed. Add vanilla, molasses, and eggs, and mix in. Scrape down the sides of the bowl, then add the brown sugar. Blend mixture lightly to a coarse texture.

With the mixer on low speed, add the dry ingredients all at once. Carefully scrape down the sides and bottom of the mixing bowl, making certain the batter is incorporated into

the flour mixture. Blend until the ingredients are combined. Do not overmix. Use the "touch test" to check the moisture balance of the dough.

Yield: approximately 7 dozen cookies.

18

Bobby Socks Scotchies

A melt-in-your-mouth butterscotch-flavored cookie, sufficient for a wild frenzy of '50s shapes such as white sport coats, saddle shoes, hamburgers, and roller skates.

8½ cups flour
1 teaspoon salt
2 teaspoons baking soda
¼ cup salted butter, room temperature
1 cup butter-flavored vegetable shortening
1½ cups granulated sugar
1½ cups brown sugar, packed
3 medium eggs
2 teaspoons LorAnn butterscotch flavoring
2 teaspoons pure vanilla
¾ cups reduced-fat buttermilk

Measure and sift flour, salt, and baking soda into a large bowl. With a wire whisk, thoroughly mix together the dry ingredients. Set aside.

Cream together the butter and vegetable shortening until well-blended. Stir in the sugars and mix lightly. Mix in the eggs, butterscotch flavoring, and vanilla. Scrape down the sides of the bowl as needed. Add the buttermilk and blend lightly, leaving the texture grainy.

Carefully add all the dry ingredients at once. Mix on low speed, scraping down the sides and bottom of the bowl to make certain all the batter is incorporated into the flour mixture. Blend until the ingredients form a ball of dough. Do not overmix. Use the "touch test" to check the moisture balance of the dough.

Yield: approximately 7 dozen cookies.

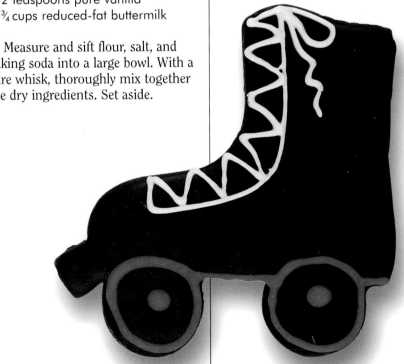

The recipe for **Cherry Chocolate Cokies is** for re-creating '50s records, poodles, and men's roller skates.

7¾ cups flour
2 teaspoons baking soda
1 teaspoon salt
1 cup butter-flavored vegetable shortening
⅓ cup unsalted butter, room temperature
3½ cups sugar
2¼ cups unsweetened cocoa powder, sifted
3 medium eggs
1 teaspoon LorAnn cherry flavoring
1 teaspoon pure vanilla extract
¾ cup cola, any brand
⅓ cup commercial sour cream

Measure and sift flour, baking soda, and salt into a large bowl. Mix the dry ingredients together with a wire whisk and set aside.

Cream together the shortening and butter. Add sugar and sifted cocoa; mix to a grainy stage. Add the eggs, cherry flavoring, vanilla, cola, and sour cream; then mix together until blended.

Add the dry ingredients all at once. Scrape down the sides and bottom of the bowl, making certain all the flour is incorporated into the batter. Mix on low speed to a ball of dough. Do not over-mix. Use the "touch test" to check the moisture balance of the dough.

Yield: approximately 6½ dozen cookies.

Cherry Chocolate Frosting

Great for '50s records, poodle dogs, saddle-shoe accents, and roller skates.

(1) 32-ounce bag confectioners' sugar, sifted
1 cup unsweetened cocoa powder
⅛ teaspoon salt
½ cup water
½ cup fat-free evaporated milk
½ cup Eagle Brand Fat-Free Sweetened Condensed Milk
1 teaspoon vanilla
¼ teaspoon LorAnn cherry flavoring

Sift together the confectioners' sugar and cocoa. Measure and place the salt, water, evaporated milk, sweetened condensed milk, vanilla, and cherry flavoring in a container. Heat in microwave or on a stove top just until bubbles appear on the inside of the container. Stir the contents and add to the confectioners' sugar. Mix on medium speed until the frosting is smooth and creamy. Place desired amounts of frosting into individual containers for coloring. Keep frosting covered at all times.

Yield: 3 cups of frosting.

Boogie-Woogie Butterscotch Frosting

Boogie to the beat of "Bulldog" as you mix up this smoothie sweet confection!

(1) 32-ounce bag confectioners' sugar, sifted
⅛ teaspoon salt
¼ cup water
¼ cup white corn syrup
¼ cup fat-free evaporated skimmed milk
¼ cup Eagle Brand Fat-Free Sweetened Condensed Milk
½ teaspoon LorAnn butterscotch flavoring

Sift the confectioners' sugar into a large mixing bowl. Measure the salt, water, corn syrup, evaporated milk, Eagle Brand Milk, and butterscotch flavoring; place in a container. Heat liquid in the microwave or on a stove top about 2 minutes or until bubbles appear on the inside of the container. Stir the contents and add to confectioners' sugar. Mix on medium speed until the frosting is smooth and creamy. Place desired amounts of frosting into individual containers for coloring. Keep frosting covered at all times.

Yield: 2¾ cups of frosting.

Royal Icing

A favorite and fun-to-make frosting recipe suitable for all '50s cookie shapes! It's yummy, too!

2 teaspoons white vanilla
¾ cup warm water
(1) 32-ounce package powdered sugar, sifted
¼ cup plus 2 tablespoons meringue powder

Note: *Make certain the mixing bowl is grease-free or the meringue won't form peaks.*

Add white vanilla to the water in the measuring cup. Sift the powdered sugar and meringue powder into a large mixing bowl. Add the liquid and beat on medium speed for about 6 to 7 minutes. Do not overbeat or the icing becomes stiff, opaque, and hard to work.

Note: *Royal icing dries to a matte finish. If you prefer a shiny surface, add 2 or 3 drops of glycerin, which can be purchased at most drugstores.*

Place the icing in lidded containers for coloring when ready. Keep containers covered at all times. If frosting is too thick, dilute with small amounts of warm water until the desired consistency is achieved. To thicken frosting for the piping bag, stir in sifted confectioners' sugar 1 tablespoon at a time. Make a practice batch of royal icing to learn the feel of the frosting. This frosting keeps for two weeks refrigerated in a tightly covered container.

Yield: about 6 cups of frosting.

Rolling out cookie dough between two sheets of plastic wrap is a different technique offering many advantages. It eliminates the need to add flour because the plastic wrap prevents the dough from sticking to the rolling pin, making it possible to utilize every crumb of scrap dough. Handling a full sheet of dough is easy, and removing cutout shapes from the rectangle of dough becomes a breeze. For professional results, carefully follow the instructions on page 24 for rolling out the dough before chilling, and use plastic wrap as directed.

Chilling Tips

After mixing the dough, wipe the countertop with a damp cloth to help the plastic wrap stick. Cut a sheet of extra wide plastic wrap (you may overlap two sheets to create the extra width) and smooth it onto the damp counter.

Divide the dough into three parts. Place a mound of dough onto the plastic wrap and, with your hands, flatten the mound to a 1-inch-thick rectangle fitting within the sheet of plastic. Place another sheet of plastic wrap over the top and apply the rolling pin to smooth out the dough to about ½-inch thickness. This step is important; it is much easier to roll out the dough while it is at room temperature.

Be sure to seal the ends of the plastic wrap around the edges to prevent dough from drying out. Place the plastic-enclosed rectangle of dough on a flat 12 x 15-inch cookie sheet. Repeat the process with the other two portions of dough, stacking the plastic-wrapped rectangles of cookie dough on top of each other on one cookie sheet. Refrigerate the dough for approximately one hour.

When ready, remove one rectangle of dough to work with; keep remaining dough refrigerated until ready to use.

Tip: Plastic wrap also works great for rolling-out perfect pie crust.

Rolling-out Tips

When the dough is chilled, remove one sheet of the plastic-wrapped dough from the refrigerator and place it on a damp counter. Release the rolled edges of the plastic wrap from around the rectangle of dough and smooth out the plastic wrap.

Roll out the dough between the two layers of plastic starting from the center and working outward by using short gentle strokes. (If the dough is very cold and not responding, allow it to sit a few minutes to become more pliable.)

As you are working the dough outward, the plastic wrap may become wrinkled. To remove the wrinkles, simply lift the plastic, smooth it out, and place it back over the rectangle of dough. To remove wrinkles from the underside, hold both layers of the plastic wrap and flip the plastic-encased sheet of dough; then straighten the plastic wrap and continue rolling.

Rotate the rolling pin as you work to prevent the dough from splitting around the edges. Roll out the rectangle of dough to around ⅜-inch uniform thickness.

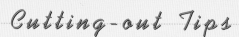

Cutting-out Tips

Lightly grease the cookie sheets or, to save cleanup time, cover the bottom of each cookie sheet with parchment paper.

For professional results, be sure the dough is perfectly smooth before you begin to cut out cookie shapes. Remove the top layer of plastic wrap.

To cut each design, place the cutter down firmly—flat on the dough—and give it a wiggle back and forth. The movement makes the dough come away from the inside edges of the cutter and it is easier to remove the cutter without breaking the cookie shape. Cut out all the shapes by placing the cutter as closely as possible to each previously cut shape.

To lift the cut-out shape, use your right hand to raise the edge of the bottom layer of plastic. Gently slip your left hand under the plastic wrap, and with the tips of your fingers, push upward on the edges of the cookie shape from underneath, breaking the cut edges loose from the plastic wrap. Use the fingers of your right hand to gently lift the cut-out cookie shape away from the dough. Place the cookies at least 1 inch apart on the cookie sheet so they do not expand and grow together as they bake. Repeat until all the cut-out shapes are removed from the rectangle of dough.

If the cutter has narrow places in the design, use the point of a small knife to gently push the dough down inside the narrow part as you lift away the cookie cutter.

If a cookie loses one of its parts, mend it by dampening the broken edges of the dough with a little water and carefully patting it back together again. The moisture helps the broken piece to seal into place during baking.

If a shape becomes distorted when you move it onto the cookie sheet, use a spatula or a knife edge to straighten the cookie. To assure a professionally finished product, carefully remove dough crumbs from the edges of the cookie shapes before baking.

After the primary shapes are cut out, you may use a mini-cutter for the remaining dough.

If you're working in large quantities, cut out all the designs from one cookie-cutter shape at once to get the maximum number of shapes from a rectangle of dough.

After cutting out shapes, knead the scraps of leftover dough into a smooth ball. Place the dough on a sheet of plastic wrap and flatten it with your hand. Cover and smooth the top of the dough with the rolling pin. Rest dough in the refrigerator for 15 minutes, then roll out. Since additional flour is not required, every scrap of dough can be used for cookies.

Note: *All recipes from* Wild, Wild West Cowboy Cookies *cookbook may be used interchangeably with recipes from this book.*

27

Baking Tips

To prevent the cookies from losing their shape, place the cut-out cookies on cool pans. (Cookie sheets cool quickly by running cold water over the back of the pans.) Bake the cookies at 350° F., one sheet at a time, on the middle rack of the oven. Although oven temperatures vary slightly, cookies are usually baked in 7 to 8 minutes. Cookies are done when you touch the center lightly and it springs back. The edges may appear slightly golden. Do not overbake, as cookies tend to become more breakable when overcooked.

After cookies are removed from the oven, allow them to set for one minute, then carefully transfer cookies with a spatula to cool on a flat surface. When cool, the cookies are ready to decorate.

G rowing up in the 1950s gave me a blueprint for cookie shapes unforgettably etched in my mind. It's been fun designing imaginative ways to decorate the cookies featured in this *Wild, Wild 1950s Cookies* book, and fun to share with you. For the most dramatic effects, mix brilliant colors of frosting for dipping on background colors and filling piping tubes. Bright coloring emphasizes the details that give your cookies personality and lifelike charm! Let your imagination jitterbug! Remember: light and dark contrasts create the most striking effects.

FUN IDEAS

You are encouraged to take the following ideas to another level, and when you create a clever new way, pass it on to all of us. As one of my new cookie-cutter collector friends said to me, "It's about caring and sharing."

Fabulous '50s Food

P op bottles" can be cola, orange, cherry, or root beer, or some of each flavor! And frost your cookie "ice-cream sodas" in vanilla, chocolate, strawberry, or butterscotch. Finish off with a dash of "whipped cream," a few chocolate sprinkles, and don't forget the cherry on top!

Before baking, brush the rounded top of your "hamburger bun" with cream or a light egg wash (beat 1 tablespoon of water into an egg white; brush on lightly); then sprinkle on sesame seeds to make it look more real. Make the meat patty of brown-tinted frosting (butterscotch or royal icing), and use a leaf piping tip to create wavy edges of green lettuce. Pipe a line of red and yellow frosting to look like mustard and ketchup.

To complement your cookie hamburgers, cut lots of ¼-inch-wide strips in various lengths of cookie dough to resemble "french fries." Sprinkle the strips with sugar before baking; they look just like real fries with salt! Pile a stack of french fries next to the decorated hamburgers, add a squirt of red frosting for ketchup, sit back and listen to the ooohs and aaahs!

From the shoe-shaped cutter, create "blue suede shoes," "white bucks," and "black- or brown-'n'-white saddle shoes."

30

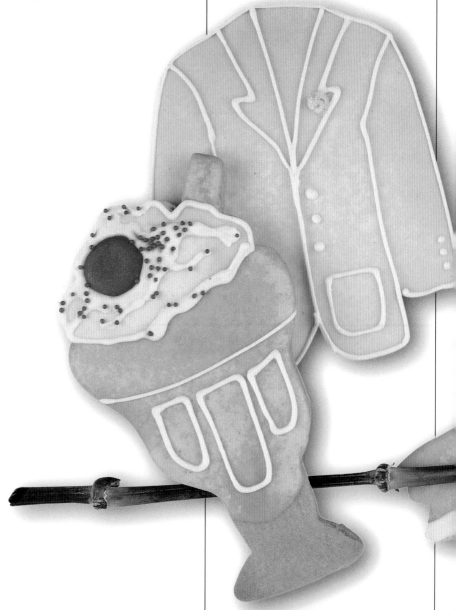

And remember to put a pink carnation on the "white sport coat." Another clever trick is to make a straight cut to remove the curved bottom of the sport coat, then frost and decorate it to look like a letter sweater in your own class colors.

Color your "poodle skirts" black, green, red, or pink—we wore them in all colors and with lots of stand-out petticoats. Decorate the border of the skirt with musical notes or records. Poodle dogs were all the rage in the 1950s, especially pink ones! Use silver dragées for make-believe "rhinestone" dog collars. (Years ago in Amarillo, Texas, I saw two women dressed in clothes that matched their carefully dyed, bouncy poodle dogs, a vanity of the times.)

P aint the '57 Chevy coupe cookie any color of frosting you wish; my favorite is a white top and a red body! Brush on a few strokes of silver Luster Dust (see p. 45) to emphasize the chrome fins and bumpers. For me, the T-bird is always pink because that was the color of Sydney Lou's car! White-wall the tires and brush silver Luster Dust on the chrome door handles.

You can use a biscuit cutter to create a clock and decorate it with a "Rock Around the Clock" theme, or make signs decorated with '50s symbols. Cut rectangles of dough and create television sets and "sugar shacks." Put lots of frosting detail on for fun. See illustrations on cookie transfers, page 44.

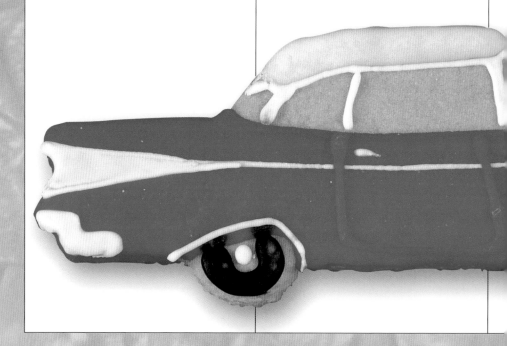

Cherry Chocolate Cokies dough is the right flavor and color for making three-speed records. With a biscuit cutter, cut out small, medium, and large circles. A drinking straw is great for making the hole for the 78 speed; select a wider circle to cut out centers on the 45s. Put colored labels on all of them, and pipe on song titles for fun. See illustrations on cookie transfers, page 44.

Jukeboxes have lots of bright-colored glass. While frosting is soft, sprinkle on Edible Glitter to give that neon-like reflection. Electric guitars came in all colors, some are even two-toned, so make 'em wild! Edible Glitter is great for shiny contrasts. Brush on chrome and brass with silver or gold Luster Dust!

Supplies

Before you begin to decorate your cookies, prepare your workspace:

- Organize plenty of working area close to the kitchen sink with good light.

- Gather plenty of clean damp cloths for wiping up frosting.

- Use spatulas, ordinary dinnerware knives, or butter knives to spread the frosting.

- Have these items on hand: waxed paper, wide plastic wrap, cookie baking pans, and large racks.

- Purchase powdered food coloring, Edible Glitter, Luster Dust, disposable decorating bags, tips, rings, and coupler bases at craft or kitchen stores, or see the Finding Sources list for ordering supplies on page 45.

- Invest in a leaf tip, a star tip, and six round metal tips in sizes 2, 3, and 4.

- To make it easy to change tips, assemble the piping tube and place the metal tip on the outside of the plastic tube/coupler, then attach the ring.

- Fill at least six piping bags in brilliant colors to pipe on contrasting frosting details.

Coloring Tips

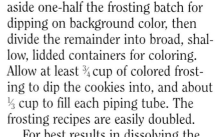

It is advisable to mix and color your frosting the day before you decorate cookies. The colors tend to intensify, and they need several hours to completely dissolve.

Purchase powdered food colors to mix brilliant shades of frosting. Set

aside one-half the frosting batch for dipping on background color, then divide the remainder into broad, shallow, lidded containers for coloring. Allow at least ¾ cup of colored frosting to dip the cookies into, and about ⅓ cup to fill each piping tube. The frosting recipes are easily doubled.

For best results in dissolving the colored powder, gently run hot water over the top of the container of white frosting, then quickly pour it off. A thin film of water remains over the top. Sprinkle the selected colored powder over the frosting to quickly absorb into the film of liquid. Stir until a uniform color of frosting is achieved. A rule of thumb applies to the coloring process: add ½ teaspoon of powdered color to ½ cup of frosting and stir well. Continue to add powdered color in small amounts until you reach the desired shade.

An edible product called Luster Dust lends a rich sheen for special metallic effects. To apply it dry, carefully brush on with a fine paintbrush, or mix it with a few drops of clear extract, such as white vanilla or almond. Measure ½ teaspoon of Luster Dust in a very small container and add the liquid by the drop until you reach a soft consistency. Paint on "chrome" accents. Luster Dust can also be mixed with alcohol such as white rum or vodka.

Note: *In a pinch, you may color low-fat commercial frosting and use it according to the directions in the book. Be aware that commercial frosting does not "set up" as well, so you must allow a longer drying time. For best results, it is advisable not to layer or ship cookies decorated with commercial frosting.*

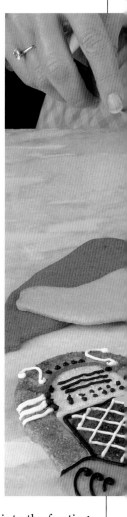

Always handle the cookies gently, as they are breakable. Be aware that extensions on the cookie shapes, such as the legs on the poodle, need to be kept flat to prevent breakage. Avoid placing any torque on fragile shapes. To lift a cookie, place the thumb and middle finger on the edges of the cookie's widest point, raise it straight up, and handle the cookie carefully between your thumb and middle finger.

Dipping cookies into the background frosting is a technique I developed to use in my home kitchen because it was faster than spreading frosting, and the results are much

36

prettier. Applying professional-looking background colors is the most critical step in cookie decorating, and a few tips can make the task go more smoothly. Decorating cookies is made easier if all the background colors are applied at one sitting and given time to "set up" before adding piping details.

Select a container with a surface broad enough to hold the cookie. Background frosting is soft and must be stirred frequently. When not in use, cover the container to prevent the formation of sugar crystals.

To dip the cookie into the frosting, hold the cookie in your left hand between your thumb and middle finger, and gently dip the surface into the desired color of frosting. Move the cookie back and forth two times to coat with frosting, then lift it out. As you raise the cookie out of the frosting, angle the cookie slightly downward, allowing the excess frosting to run off. With your right hand, use a flat spatula or knife blade to gently smooth the frosting across the surface, allowing the excess to fall back into the container. With a clean

knife edge, run the blade around the entire outside edge of the cookie to remove any runs and to seal frosting around the edges. (Edible Glitter or sprinkles must be applied at this point.) Be sure to correct frosting runs before the frosting sets up. Place the cookie on a large cookie rack or a sheet of waxed paper to set up.

As you work with the background colors, maintain the soft consistency of the frosting, stirring often to prevent sugar crystals from forming. If sugar crystals appear, stop decorating. Dissolve the crystals by gently adding

½ inch of very hot water to cover the entire surface of the frosting in its container. Allow the hot water to remain for ten seconds and then pour off the entire amount. The crystals are dissolved and the thin film of water at the top is often sufficient liquid to stir the frosting back to the desirable consistency for dipping.

While the frosting is soft, check to see if excess frosting has run over the edge of the cookie shape. If a frosting run occurs, use care in lifting the cookie off the rack. To raise it without marring the frosting, slip a spatula underneath the cookie, raise it, and place the cookie in your outstretched left palm. Holding the cookie in your hand, use your right hand to remove the excess by running a clean knife edge around the outside edge. (You can also use your finger to remove the frosting run and seal the frosting to the edge.) The goal is to have a smooth frosted surface and clean edge to each cookie. Remember, practice makes perfect.

After dipping on the background colors and correcting the edges for runs, place the cookies on clean waxed paper or cookie racks and allow the surface to dry for at least four hours. Make certain the background frosting is completely dry before applying the frosting details or the colors will run together and mar the appearance of your cookies.

Piped-on Details

The frosting used to fill the piping tube must be thicker than the frosting mixed for the background colors. To thicken the reserved frosting for piping, add sifted confectioners' sugar by the tablespoon until folds of the frosting are observable when you stir through the mixture. A fairly stiff consistency is most desirable. The ideal consistency is achieved when piping flows from the tube, adheres to the background surface of the cookie, and holds its shape.

To fill the frosting tube easily, fold back the wide end of the piping tube (as you would cuff a pair of bobby socks) and place the metal-tipped end inside a tall glass, allowing the edges of the folded tube to overhang on the outside of the glass. Spread the opening and use a spoon to place the frosting into the plastic tube. Remove the tube from the glass, shake the frosting down, then use your hands to squeeze the frosting to the very bottom until the frosting begins to flow from the decorating tip. Gather the ends of the tube and twist tightly

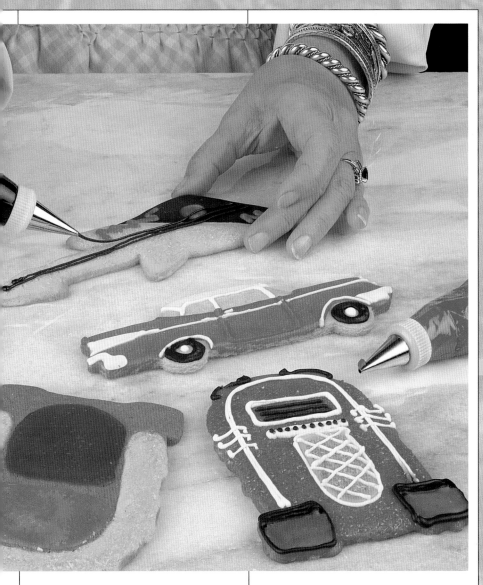

to hold the frosting in place. Secure the end with a baggy twist.

When applying piping detail, squeeze the frosting tube from the twisted end of the bag. As you work, twist the bag to take up the slack and adjust the baggy tie if necessary. If the frosting is too thick to squeeze from the piping tube, run a little hot water over the outside of the plastic bag to soften it. If the frosting in the

filled tube is too runny, chill it in the refrigerator for a few minutes.

Try this clever trick for practicing piping designs: wrap a piece of clear plastic wrap over a cookie; pipe the design onto the clear plastic; continue to practice, tossing the practice plastic wrap away and trying again until you feel satisfied with handling the piping tube. With a little practice you can become very proficient.

STORING

The pleasure of making decorated cookies is made easier when the cookies are baked in advance and stored or frozen for decorating at a later date. Undecorated, the cookies freeze very well for several months. Place them in an airtight container with sheets of plastic wrap or waxed paper and cut-to-fit pieces of poster board or cardboard between each layer to prevent breakage.

Note: *To preserve each cookie flavor, freeze and/or store Bobby Sock Scotchies, Cherry Chocolate Cokies, and Jukebox Gingies in separate containers.*

Packed in the same manner, frosted cookies store well up to two weeks in a cool place out of direct sunlight. Light and heat may mottle some of the frosting colors. It is best not to freeze cookies after they are frosted as moisture causes the colors to bleed and distort their professional appearance.

If cookies, frosted or unfrosted, become too brittle and break easily, experiment in your climate with storing them in a covered plastic container with one or two slices of fresh white bread. Place the bread slices on the bottom of the container and lay the cookie racks over the bread. Add a single layer of cookies on the rack; do not stack cookies as the frosting colors may run from the moisture in the bread slices. Close the lid and in a few hours the cookies become soft without any change in flavor.

SHIPPING

All of the cookies from the recipes in the book ship well if carefully packed. Select an appropriate-size box and line the bottom with bubble wrap to absorb shock. Line the inside of the box with plastic wrap, allowing it to extend past the edges. (Wrapping each cookie in plastic wrap is optional.) To prevent breakage, place cookies flat and close together, making certain the cookies do not overlap. Place more plastic wrap over the top, add another piece of cut-to-fit bubble wrap, then poster board or cardboard.

Continue filling the box in this manner, leaving space at the top for a final layer of bubble wrap. When full, bring the outside edges of the plastic wrap together to enclose all the layers of cookies inside to keep them fresh during shipping. Add a final layer of bubble wrap, ensuring there is no movement inside the box; then cover and tape or tie the box closed. Add an additional layer of bubble wrap around the package; place it inside a corrugated cardboard box with additional paper packing to make it fit snugly inside.

Cookies hold through shipping overnight express, UPS Ground, or U.S. Priority Mail.

Tuda Libby Crews has taught the art of decorating *wild, wild cookies* in workshops and demonstrations from Nevada to New York. She has appeared on national and local television shows, and presented programs to convention groups. When time permits, she and her husband, Jack, hitch up their antique chuck wagon and compete in authentic chuck wagon cook-offs, a passion they have shared for many years.

With great pride, Tuda brings her imaginative and original collection of trademarked cutters to cookie bakers and cookie-cutter collectors worldwide through her home-based business. All cookie cutters featured in *Wild, Wild 1950s Cookies* are accessible to home bakers and collectors. You may order the cutters from her Web address at www.wildwestcookies.com or by photocopying the order form at the back of the book. Call the toll-free number (1-888) 277-0294 to send a fax or leave a voice mail. To fulfill her goal of sharing cookie-making secrets with people who love to bake and decorate cookies, plans are in the works to produce a video for cookie lovers to use at home.

Both *Wild, Wild West Cowboy Cookies* and *Wild, Wild 1950s Cookies* (the second in her Wild, Wild series) are published by Gibbs Smith, Publisher. The books are available at major book stores all over the United States, and by calling Gibbs Smith, Publisher, at (1-800) 748-5439.

Trace onto baking parchment, cut out templates, and transfer onto rolled-out dough. Pipe frosting details as indicated.

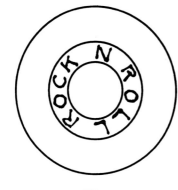

PRODUCTS

The Baker's Catalogue®
P.O. Box 876
Norwich, VT 05055

(1-800) 827-6836
Fax: (1-800) 343-3002

Sweet Celebrations, Inc.™
P.O. Box 39426
Edina MN 55439

(1-800) 328-6722
Fax: (612) 943-1688
E-mail:
   sweetcel@maidofscandinavia.com
Website: www.sweetc.com

LorAnn Oils, Inc.
P.O. Box 22009
Lansing MI 48909

(1-800) 248-1302
Fax: (517) 882-0507
Website: www.lorannoils.com

Creative Cake, Candy & Cookie Supplies
9967 Clark Drive
Northglenn CO 80221

(303) 450-2624
E-mail: ccandc@Juno.com

CONCERTS

The Fireballs
P.O. Box 1204
Raton NM 87740-1204

Ph/Fax: (505) 445-9739

The Crickets

Formed in 1956 by Buddy Holly and J. I. Allison, the Crickets are still performing today. For more information, contact

The Crickets
Gold Mountain Entertainment
1514 South Street, Suite 100
Nashville TN 37212

(615) 255-9000
Fax: (615) 255-9001

Hot August Nights

Come celebrate the cars and the music of the '50s and the '60s. More than 175,000 people descend on northern Nevada to pay homage to the "Happy Days." For more information, contact

Hot August Nights
1455 Deming Way #11
Reno / Sparks NV 89431

(702) 356-1956
Fax: (702) 356-1957

RECORDINGS

Dundee Music
Box 926
Clovis NM 88101

(505) 356-6422

Collector's Choice Music
P.O. Box 838
Itasca IL 60143-0838

(1-800) 923-1122
Fax: (630) 775-3340

45

ATTENTION ALL COOKIE LOVERS!

P rofessional instruction on baking and decorating Wild, Wild 1950s Cookies is made fun and educational in presentations specially designed for entertainment or in-store promotion. Tuda "brings out the child" in participants as she teaches easy-to-learn techniques for creating home-baked and beautifully decorated cookies. Audience participation is always encouraged. Skills acquired in cookie-decorating demonstrations and workshops delight family and friends. Books and cookie cutters are available for sale at locations. For arrangements, please contact the author at the following address:

Tuda Libby Crews
Wild West Cutters
P.O. Box 1804
Cheyenne WY 82003-1804

Toll-free fax: (1-888) 277-0294
E-mail: info@wildwestcookies.com
Website: www.wildwestcookies.com

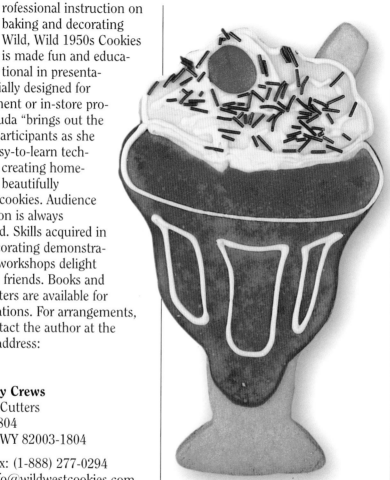

46

COLLECTOR'S EDITION OF WILD, WILD 1950s COOKIE CUTTERS

It's time to turn on the jukebox and jive and bop your way through these simple, delicious recipes that will set your '50s nostalgia in full swing! Choose from three toe-tapping recipes—Jukebox Gingies, Bobby Socks Scotchies, and Cherry Chocolate Cokies—then turn out cookies shaped like these '50s icons:

Jukebox
Poodle Dog
Ice-Cream Soda
White Sport Coat
Poodle Skirt
'57 Chevy
'57 T-bird
Roller Skate
Blue Suede Shoe
Hamburger
Pop Bottle
Electric Guitar

Elenna Firme designed the captivating cookie-cutter shapes from the '50s era to charm the most discriminating cookie bakers.

Michael Bonne adds his mastery of fine handcrafted copper work to create three of the original cookie-cutter designs. Using antique hand- and foot-operated tools, Michael's time-honored tradition in creating quality copper work is unsurpassable, and each copper cutter carries his mark as well as Tuda's logo.

A '50s frenzy of nine quality, originally designed outline cutters complete this nostalgic collection of cookie shapes. All cutters are imprinted with Tuda's trademark and are available only by ordering from the following sources:

U.S. Mail:
Wild West Cutters
P.O. Box 1804
Cheyenne WY 82003

Toll-free fax: (1-888) 277-0294

Website: www.wildwestcookies.com

47

WILD 1950's COOKIE-CUTTER ORDER FORM

ORDER BY: **PLEASE PRINT LEGIBLY**

Name

Address

City   State   Zip

Home phone

Evening phone

Be sure to fill in form completely. Include physical address for UPS delivery.

SHIPPING ADDRESS (IF DIFFERENT):

Name   c/o

Address

City   State   Zip

METHOD OF PAYMENT

❏ Check or money order enclosed

Visa or MC: card number   exp. date

Signature as shown on credit card

ORDER INFORMATION:

Item Number	Descriptions	How Many?	Price Each	Total Price
CE20	Jukebox		$16.95	
CE21	Poodle Dog		$13.95	
CE22	Ice-Cream Soda		$14.95	
23	White Sport Coat		$6.50	
24	Poodle Skirt		$6.50	
25	'57 Chevy		$6.50	
26	'57 T-Bird		$6.50	
27	Roller Skate		$6.50	
28	Blue Suede Shoe		$6.50	
29	Hamburger		$6.50	
30	Pop Bottle		$6.50	
31	Electric Guitar		$6.50	
		TOTAL FOR MERCHANDISE		
		Wyoming Shipments add 5%.		
		Add applicable sales tax.		
		Add for Shipping and Handling (see chart below)		
		TOTAL AMOUNT ENCLOSED		

SHIPPING AND HANDLING CHARGES:
UPS is the standard methods for continental USA shipments.
U.S. PARCEL POST is the standard method for Hawaii, Alaska.
(USA by request)

ORDER TOTAL	Surface 9–12 Working Days	UPS Blue Label 3 Days	UPS Red Label 2 Working Days
$00.00 to $30.00	$4.75	$6.75	$16.75
$30.01 to $60.00	$6.95	$8.95	$18.95
$60.01 to $100.00	$8.75	$10.75	$20.75
$100.01 to $200.00	$10.25	$12.25	$22.25
Over $200.00	$11.75	$13.75	$23.75

WILD 1950S CUTTERS
P.O. Box 1804
Cheyenne WY 82003-1804

Place orders to this toll-free fax:
(1-888) 277-0294
Website: **www.wildwestcookies.com**

For further information, write to this
E-mail address:
info@wildwestcookies.com

TUDA™ LLC

ALLOW THREE WEEKS FOR DELIVERY

48